MW01152851

Writing Workbook for Kids with Dyslexia

100 activities to improve writing and reading skills of dyslexic children

VOLUME 4

Brain Child

Copyright 2020 - All Rights Reserved

Contents of this book may not be reproduced, duplicated or transmitted without direct written permission from the author.

Under no circumstances will any legal responsibility or blame be held against the publisher for any reparation, damages or monetary loss due to information herein, either directly or indirectly.

Legal Notice:

You cannot amend, distribute, sell, use, quote or paraphrase any part of the contents within this book without the consent of the author.

Disclaimer Notice:

Please note that information contained within this document is educational and entertainment serves only for educationaly entertainment purposes. No warranties of any kind are expressed or implied. Readers acknowledge that the author is not engaging in the rendering of legal, financial, medical or professional advice.

Table of contents

Table of contents

Table of contents

Table of contents

Table of contents

Table of contents

INTRODUCTION

Visit www.brainchildgrowth.com and download 25 free extra activities.

Dyslexia is a learning disorder. It can be said that a person is dyslexic when they have difficulties reading and understanding what is written.

When a child has dyslexia, it is much more difficult to decode the letters and read fluently. That is why these children often have difficulties following the class.

Dyslexia can be worked to improve the child's reading, writing and reading comprehension. The best way to work on these exercises with your child is to create a routine and work on one or two exercises each day.

Exercises to practice writing are covered in this volume and then a complementary activity to practice with the letters learned.

Never put excessive pressure on the child. Patience should be our word mantra. Keep in mind that for the child an exercise that you consider easy is very hard for them.

Focus on the child's small advances. Power your effort and less your results. Do everything you can so that they don't feel bad. Keep in mind that the child is making a great effort.

When we suspect that our child may be dyslexic, we can do a series of activities that will improve their literacy level. Whether in the end, the diagnosis is confirmed or discarded, it will still be very beneficial to facilitate their learning experience.

The important thing is to carry out this type of training before the age of 8 or 9, preferably during the last year of pre-school and the first year of primary school, without taking into account that from school there is still no warning.

In any case, we cannot wait for the diagnosis to be confirmed because we will have missed the best time to intervene and prepare the child to learn to read, and we will have a serious problem if they start 3rd grade and we have not yet intervened the dyslexia, since the increase in school demands will make the problem visible.

In this book and the other volumes of BrainChild, you will find a multitude of resources to work with dyslexia both at school and at home. The exercises have been carried out under the supervision of psychologists and educators.

SYLLABLES

The act of dividing big words down into small pieces (_syllables_) is so that they can be spelled more easily.

Types of Syllables

OPEN CV	The vowel is usually long and has a syllable ending with a single vowel.	po-ta-to
CLOSED VC	The vowel is usually short and has a syllable ending with a consonant.	sand-wich
SILENT E V-E	The vowel is usually long in the middle and has a syllable ending with a silent 'e'.	cake
VOWEL TEAM VV	A syllable containing two vowels, one is long and the other one is silent.	boat
DIPHTHONG VV	It has two vowels and both vowels forme a new vowel sound.	cloud
R CONTROLLED VR	The vowel and 'r' together and controlled by the letter 'r'.	burger
CONSONANT -CLE	A syllable ends with a consonant and -cle and has no vowel sound (the e at the end is silent).	apple

How **many** syllables?

Read the word and clap the syllables. Mark the correct number of syllables.

SEAHORSE
(1) (2) (3)

BALLOON
(1) (2) (3)

TRAIN
(1) (2) (3)

BIRD
(1) (2) (3)

CORN
(1) (2) (3)

STRAWBERRY
(1) (2) (3)

CUPCAKE
(1) (2) (3)

CAR
(1) (2) (3)

FLOWER
(1) (2) (3)

Syllables

Read the word and put a check mark in the correct box.

WORD	1 syllable	2 syllables	3 syllables
basket	☐	☐	☐
pumpkin	☐	☐	☐
habit	☐	☐	☐
dentist	☐	☐	☐
lobby	☐	☐	☐
umbrella	☐	☐	☐
bear	☐	☐	☐
twelve	☐	☐	☐
alphabet	☐	☐	☐
computer	☐	☐	☐
house	☐	☐	☐
bus	☐	☐	☐
caterpillar	☐	☐	☐
horse	☐	☐	☐

3

Dot the Syllables

Determine how many syllables there are and make a dot on the blank circles with a stamp.

candle   ◯ ◯ ◯ ◯

window   ◯ ◯ ◯ ◯

letter   ◯ ◯ ◯ ◯

book   ◯ ◯ ◯ ◯

elephant   ◯ ◯ ◯ ◯

star   ◯ ◯ ◯ ◯

octopus   ◯ ◯ ◯ ◯

Match two Syllables

Draw a line between 2 syllables to make the word.

tur	gle
bub	tile
can	plode
ea	cake
jung	tle
rep	ger
ex	der
pan	dle
fin	der
lad	ble

Omission of Syllables

Remove the 2nd syllable from the word and write the remaining word in the blank box.

win<u>dow</u>	→	win
cartoon	→	
pumpkin	→	
necklace	→	
jacket	→	
candle	→	
pickle	→	
inside	→	

6

Omission of Syllables

Read the words and write the 1st and 2nd syllable on the lines.

	1st syllable	2nd syllable
sister	_____	_____
mitten	_____	_____
monkey	_____	_____
pencil	_____	_____
ribbon	_____	_____

Omission of Syllables

Read the words and write the 1st syllable in the given boxes.

planet	chanted	racket
_____	_____	_____
subject	sample	cattle
_____	_____	_____
kneecap	plastic	vanish
_____	_____	_____
distance	vintage	pencil
_____	_____	_____
wagon	firehouse	jingle
_____	_____	_____

Substitution of syllables

Replace the 2nd syllable of the word with 'th'.

terrible

_____

elephant

_____

fingers

_____

president

_____

freedom

_____

butterfly

_____

reading

_____

football

_____

playground

_____

popcorn

_____

9

Substitution of syllables

Replace the 2nd syllable of the word with 'ru'.

notebook	trumpet
_____	_____
patato	monster
_____	_____
unhappy	chocolate
_____	_____
horrible	banana
_____	_____
difficult	understand
_____	_____

10

Substitution of syllables

Replace the 2nd syllable of the word with 'sh'.

stomach _____	woman _____	woman _____
asleep _____	advice _____	admire _____
object _____	gorilla _____	eagle _____
parrot _____	grapes _____	potato _____
airplane _____	mango _____	seven _____

Substitution of syllables

Replace the 2nd syllable of the word with 'ar'.

upset	clever	vehicle
_____	_____	_____
animal	flower	today
_____	_____	_____
steamer	crockery	custard
_____	_____	_____
perfect	fitness	friend
_____	_____	_____
enjoyness	children	comfort
_____	_____	_____

12

Find orally hidden Syllables

Find and match the missing syllable in the word.

f__ger	oc
s__ool	wa
cl__k	ai
ch__r	se
__tch	in
sug__	ra
hou__	ar
t__in	ch

13

Find orally hidden Syllables

Look at the picture and fill in the missing letter.

ci__us	cup__ke	cher__
alliga__r	ju__ler	ba__et
bott__	c__b	broc__li

14

Find orally hidden Syllables

Use the suffix 'ion'. Write the complete word in the given boxes.

sess____

act____

frict____

vis____

rotat____

inflat____

extens____

stat____

pollut____

vacat____

miss____

15

Find orally hidden Syllables

Add the missing syllable to form the complete word.

th →	thumb
sk →	
di →	
pa →	
br →	
fi →	
gr →	

ho →	
ic →	
ka →	
le →	
na →	
ri →	
wa →	

16

Identify repeated syllable

Underline which syllable repeats itself in both words.

dedic<u>ate</u> / hesit<u>ate</u>	bug / rug	chair / stair
purse / nurse	addition / edition	make / take
congratulate / classmate	rocket / pocket	evaporate / negotiate
fall / tall	bunch / lunch	bear / near
ostrich / spinach	each / beach	wish / dish

17

Identify repeated syllable

Write the syllable 'es' at the end of both words.

bush – bushes fox – foxes	kiss – bench –	bus – peach –
class – glass –	brush – bush –	guess – address –
witch – church –	dress – princess –	cross – fox –
itch – boss –	buzz – minus –	eyelash – watch –
mattress – index –	coach – pouch –	prefix – complex –

18

Identify repeated syllable

Highlight the syllable 'ow' found in the different words.

snow	own	know
flow	low	bow
slow	wolf	row
blow	show	grower
down	town	shown
pillow	owl	arrow
glow	fellow	hollow
bowl	yellow	below

Identify repeated syllable

Highlight the syllable 'o e' found in the different words.

phone	code	rose
globe	gotten	cope
hope	forest	broke
awoke	stone	grower
smoke	robe	close
pole	done	note
choke	mole	lobe
hottest	blotted	rocket

20

Word chain syllable

I see-I see a little thing that begins with the piece or strings of words.

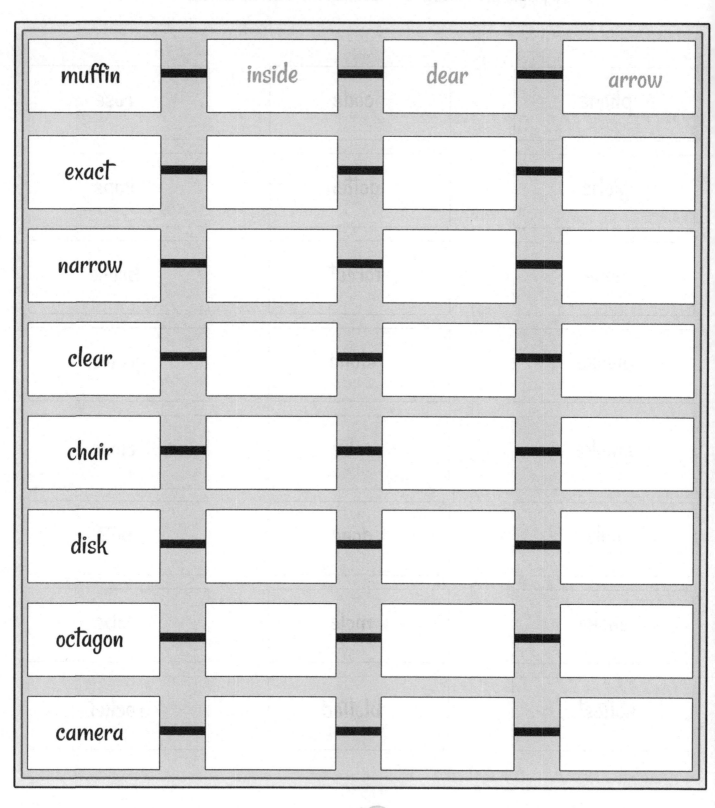

muffin	inside	dear	arrow
exact			
narrow			
clear			
chair			
disk			
octagon			
camera			

21

Word chain syllable

I see-I see a little thing that begins with the piece or strings of words.

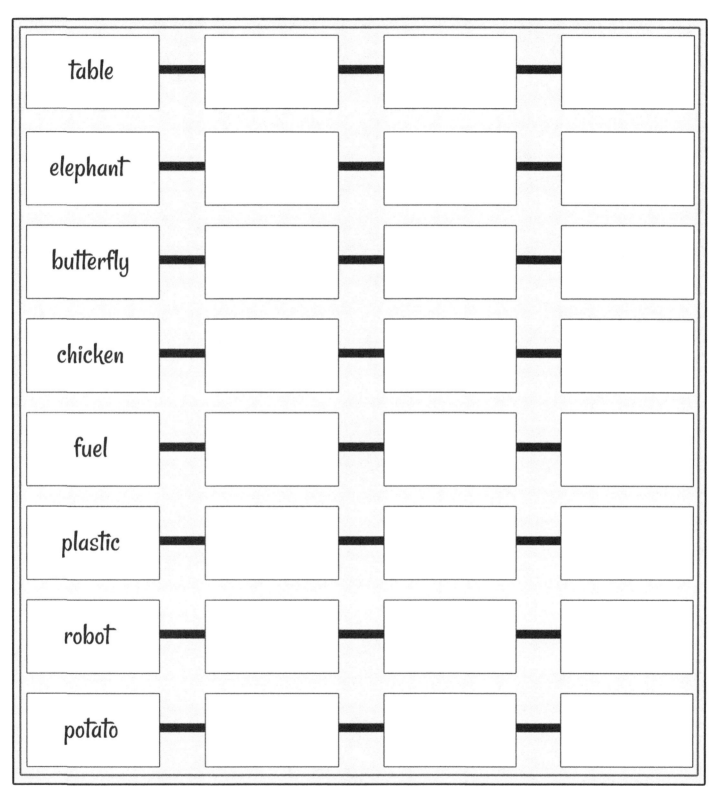

table			
elephant			
butterfly			
chicken			
fuel			
plastic			
robot			
potato			

22

Word chain syllable

I see-I see a little thing that begins with the piece or strings of words.

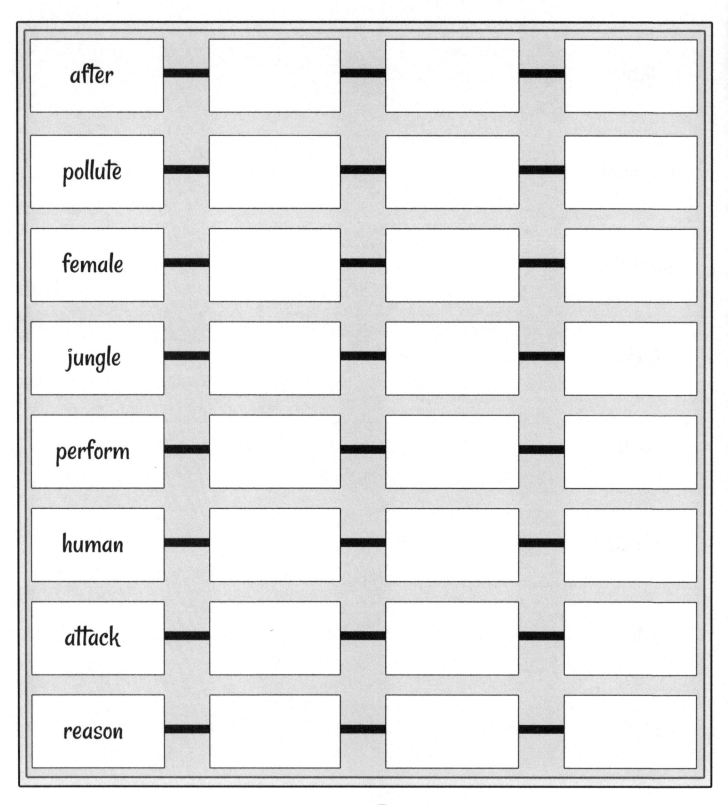

after			
pollute			
female			
jungle			
perform			
human			
attack			
reason			

23

Word chain syllable

I see–I see a little thing that begins with the piece or strings of words.

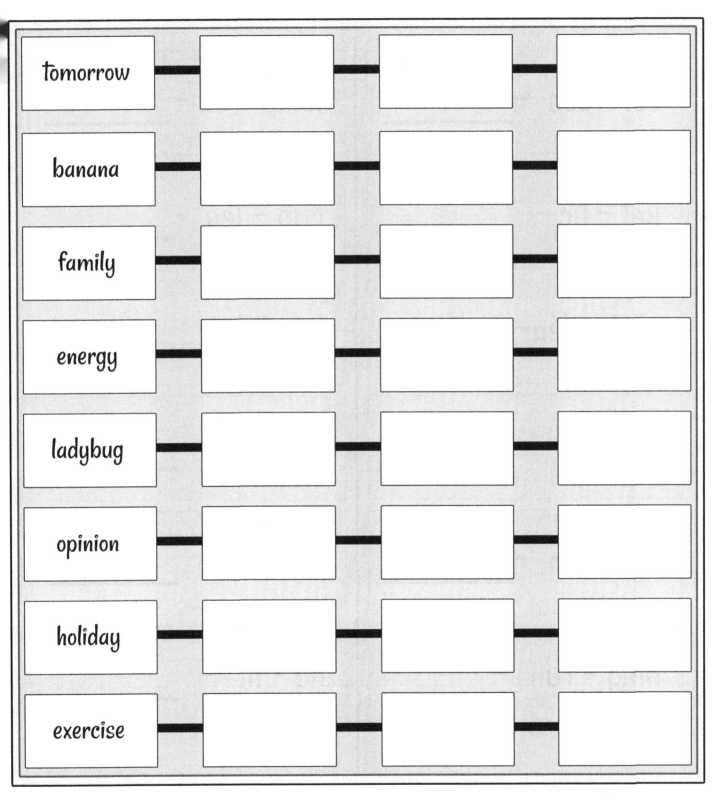

tomorrow			
banana			
family			
energy			
ladybug			
opinion			
holiday			
exercise			

24

Order the syllable

Order the syllables to form a word.

1. ool – sch – _school_

2. tract – ex – _____

3. ket – tic – _____

4. cup – tea – _____

5. cher – tea – _____

6. le – tab – _____

7. za – piz – _____

8. ten – kit – _____

9. ny – bun – _____

10. ple – ap – _____

11. ning – run – _____

12. tte – lit – _____

25

Order the syllable

Order the syllables to form a word.

1. ter – cop – heli   –   helicopter
   _____

2. pect – dis – res   –   _____

3. nes – day – wed   –   _____

4. por – im – tant   –   _____

5. cum – ber – cu   –   _____

6. ble – in – credi   –   _____

26

Order the syllable

Order the syllables to form a word.

1. der – won   – _____

2. ster – ham   – _____

3. ject – sub   – _____

4. cil – pen   – _____

5. on – wag   – _____

6. ster – ham   – _____

27

Order the syllable

Order the syllables to form a word.

1. av – ca – o – do

_____
avocado

2. cu – la – tor – cal

_____

3. for – nia – i – cal

_____

4. tor – mo – cle– cy

_____

5. oc – bin – u – lars

_____

6. un – ver – i – sity

_____

7. colo – wa – ter – rist

_____

8. ge – ref – rator – ri

_____

9. o – id – e – logy

_____

10. gi – bio – lo – cal

_____

28

Complete words **with syllable**

Read and fill in the blanks to complete the words.

elec__ti__on

__nnection

du____tion

in____ction

con____tion

a____ition

con____usion

d____ision

loc____ion

ma____cian

tran____tion

p____motion

positi____

di____sion

extensi____

co____ission

29

Complete words with syllable

Read and fill in the blanks to complete the words.

bio___gical	ut___sil
di___cting	p___moting
a___otment	ob___ction
sta___on	vi___on
___pression	fus___n
inc___sion	___mension
se___ion	missi___
act___n	subt___ction

30

Complete words **with syllable**

Read and fill in the blanks with the syllables '-le, -el, -il' to complete the words.

ang ___ le	___ el	___ il
___ le	___ el	___ il
___ le	___ el	___ il
___ le	___ el	___ il
___ le	___ el	___ il
___ le	___ el	___ il
___ le	___ el	___ il

31

Complete words **with syllable**

Read and fill in the blanks with the syllables '-ate, -able, -ing' to complete the words.

<u>calcul</u> ate	_____ able	_____ ing
_____ ate	_____ able	_____ ing
_____ ate	_____ able	_____ ing
_____ ate	_____ able	_____ ing
_____ ate	_____ able	_____ ing
_____ ate	_____ able	_____ ing
_____ ate	_____ able	_____ ing

32

Phoneme Segmentation

How many sounds does the word have?

word	phoneme	sounds
frog	f-r-o-g	4
many		
people		
right		
perfect		
pentagon		
trumpet		

33

Phoneme Segmentation

How many sounds does the word have?

Say the name of the given picture.

Write the phoneme.

Write the number of sounds.

Write the word.

Say the name of the given picture.

Write the phoneme.

Write the number of sounds.

Write the word.

34

Phoneme Segmentation

How many sounds does the word have?

5 ←	w – a – t – e – r	☐ ←	s – l – e – e – p
☐ ←	w – i – p – e	☐ ←	t – e – l – l
☐ ←	l – i – g – h – t	☐ ←	c – o – o – k
☐ ←	c – i – r – c – l – e	☐ ←	a – n – s – w – e – r
☐ ←	h – i – d – d – e – n	☐ ←	s – h – a – p – e
☐ ←	b – u – t – t – e – r	☐ ←	c – – r – e – a – t – e
☐ ←	r – e – a – s – o – n	☐ ←	m – o – n – t – h

35

Phoneme Segmentation

Find and count the sounds, and write the phoneme words in the correct box.

ink	around	wings	spread	start
put	silk	beauty	color	play
moth	sunset	fly	green	more
ready	belong	even	huge	recent
study	year	group	them	exotic
mostly	flower	bodies	fly	bright

3	4	5	6
ink			

36

Phoneme Skipping

What would remain if we removed the 2nd sound from the word?

p_lay – pay	white –	family –
paper –	group –	basket –
army –	those –	jumped –
class –	sister –	fish –
school –	tiger –	hill –
keep –	show –	carry –
rose –	trumpet –	myself –
never –	small –	warm –
always –	found –	write –
because –	thought –	along –
stored –	whole –	poster –

37

Phoneme Skipping

What would remain if we removed the 2nd sound from the word?

break –	black –	world –
shift –	plastic –	found –
often –	second –	house –
young –	close –	means –
mountain –	earth –	think –
shop –	soon –	over –
base –	really –	learn –
plant –	almost –	strike –
flower –	forest –	zebra –
devil –	those –	rabbit –
golden –	change	opinion –

Phoneme Skipping

What would remain if we removed the 2nd sound from the word?

igloo -   iloo

bread -

crab -

panda -

donkey -

iguana -

orange -

candy -

leaf -

giraffe -

39

Phoneme Skipping

What would remain if we removed the 2nd sound from the word?

raccoon –

glass –

horse –

kangaroo –

lamp –

monkey –

moon –

kite –

penguin –

mother –

40

Phoneme Substitution

Replace the 2nd sound of the word and write it.

Replace the 2nd sound of the word with the / "a" /sound.

fever   faver _____

Replace the 2nd sound of the word with the / "o" /sound.

pumpkin _____

Replace the 2nd sound of the word with the / "h" /sound.

rain _____

Replace the 2nd sound of the word with the / "r" /sound.

sheep _____

Replace the 2nd sound of the word with the / "t" /sound.

snail _____

Replace the 2nd sound of the word with the / "i" /sound.

turtle _____

Replace the 2nd sound of the word with the / "s" /sound.

umbrella _____

41

Phoneme Substitution

Replace the 2nd sound of the word and write it.

Replace the 2nd sound of the word with the / "a" / sound.

yacht _____

Replace the 2nd sound of the word with the / "e" / sound.

unicorn _____

Replace the 2nd sound of the word with the / "i" / sound.

yoghurt _____

Replace the 2nd sound of the word with the / "o" / sound.

tree _____

Replace the 2nd sound of the word with the / "u " / sound.

milk _____

Replace the 2nd sound of the word with the / "p" / sound.

world _____

Replace the 2nd sound of the word with the / "k" / sound.

zebra _____

42

Phoneme Substitution

Replace the 2nd sound of the word with the / "r" /sound.

lemon Irmon	control	apply
former	clarify	depend
exercise	select	involve
justify	focus	expand
assign	document	remove

43

Phoneme Substitution

Replace the 2nd sound of the word with the / "h" /sound.

little _____	myself _____	their _____
ready _____	question _____	against _____
begin _____	special _____	happen _____
happen _____	slowly _____	under _____
everything _____	without _____	until _____

44

Find the hidden sounds

Write the hidden phoneme or sound that is missing in the word.

bak_i_ng	harv_st	cookin_
trav_l	foot_all	bi_cuit
co_n	stuff_ng	brow_
t_rkey	fe_tival	wa_ching
ble_sed	honor_d	re_lection
gr_ce	lo_e	gra_e
s_uash	tha_ks	sa_ad

45

Find the hidden sounds

Write the hidden phoneme or sound that is missing in the word.

l_rge	g_od	r_ch
ang_y	accur_te	dama_e
arr_ve	sto_e	spea_
w_nt	beha_e	o_erate
ann_y	del_cate	br_ght
rece_ve	p_ster	wa_te
des_gn	fu_ction	dis_lay

46

Find the hidden sounds

Match the hidden phoneme or sound that is missing in the word.

l_fe	p
s_ace	s
stai_	h
fini_h	x
_uman	i
rub_er	f
e_it	b
_an	c
ja_ket	z
_ebra	r

47

Find the hidden sounds

What sound or phoneme sounds the same in the two given words?

<u>a</u>pple <u>a</u>nt	`a`	<u>ch</u>air <u>ch</u>ocolate		shark sheep	
jug joker		fish frog		market melted	
winter well		print packed		care cart	
away arm		gain grapes		potato park	
brain bat		crayon clock		shiny share	
young yacht		queen quilt		guess grass	

Auditory sound discrimination

Circle the picture with the given sound.

Circle the picture with the "L" sound.

Circle the picture with the "P" sound.

Circle the picture with the "M" sound.

Circle the picture with the "A" sound.

Circle the picture with the "S" sound.

Auditory sound discrimination

Circle the picture with the given sound.

Circle the picture with the "G" sound.

Circle the picture with the "O" sound.

Circle the picture with the "K" sound.

Circle the picture with the "F" sound.

Circle the picture with the "N" sound.

Auditory sound discrimination

Find and circle the picture with the given sound.

I see a thing that begins with the / p / sound.

I see a thing that begins with the / j / sound.

I see a thing that begins with the / h / sound.

I see a thing that begins with the / u / sound.

I see a thing that begins with the / w / sound.

Auditory sound discrimination

Find and circle the picture with the given sound.

I see a thing that begins with the / a / sound.

I see a thing that begins with the / f / sound.

I see a thing that begins with the / i / sound.

I see a thing that begins with the / c / sound.

I see a thing that begins with the / t / sound.

52

Graphemes to form words

Order the following letters to form a word.

doyb - body

uqnee - _____

hoolsc - _____

alcss - _____

irpa - _____

enifrd - _____

lbeu - _____

irdkn - _____

lemis - _____

53

Graphemes to form words

Order the following letters to form a word.

lapy - _____

kcoo - _____

ugh - _____

ept - _____

aksne - _____

nhda - _____

regne - _____

aprk - _____

nulch - _____

54

Graphemes to form words

Order the following letters to form a word.

seeche - *cheese*

ihfs -

sckos -

owlref -

llbe -

ciuje -

ndcya -

oclkc -

55

Graphemes to form words

Order the following letters to form a word.

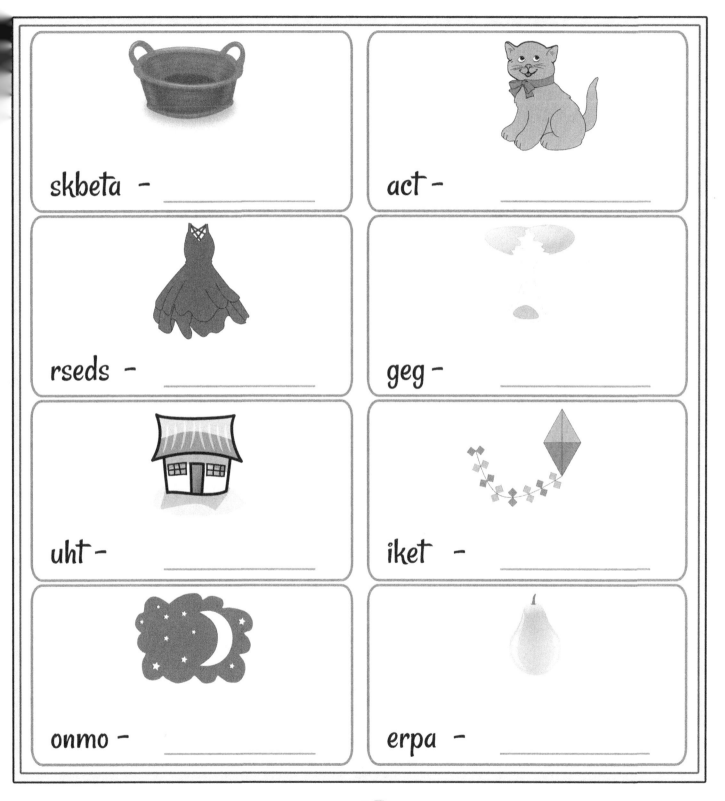

skbeta - _____

act - _____

rseds - _____

geg - _____

uht - _____

iket - _____

onmo - _____

erpa - _____

Complete words **with graphemes**

Read and complete the word with graphemes.

b<u>u</u>tterfly

p_ncake

j_lly

b_th

g_ass

f_mily

s_rub

b_nd

c_ack

t_nt

b_at

c_est

57

Complete words **with graphemes**

Read and complete the word with graphemes.

t_llest   s_nflower

h_ppy   p_ay

g_ound   d_eam

k_tten   s_ow

w_nter   f_otball

c_rrot   f_nny

58

Complete words **with graphemes**

Read and circle the correct graphemes.

	I like c_ke.	(a) m
	I see a _og.	s d
	I have a c_r.	a e
	I can p_ay.	l w
	I like m_lk	f i
	I see a g_raffe.	i u

59

Complete words **with graphemes**

Read and circle the correct graphemes.

	The _oon is in the sky.	(m) t
	This is a m_n.	e a
	Give me a b_ok	o r
	Her dress is _ink	g p
	I am a b_y.	o f
	She is my m_ther.	b o

60

Dictations of sounds

What word am I named? Write the sounds that make up a certain word.

morning – / m / / o / / r / / n / / i / / n / / g /	airplane –
elephant –	hen –
bicycle –	caterpillar –
carrot –	music –
crocodile –	monster –
notebook –	train –

61

Dictations of sounds

What word am I named? Write the sounds that make up a certain word.

chess
–

dancer
–

paper
–

violin
–

doctor
–

yellow
–

dinosaur
–

umbrella
–

fruits
–

vegetable
–

spring
–

gun
–

62

Dictations of sounds

Draw a line to connect the sounds that make up the name of the picture.

sh   br

Dictations of sounds

Draw a line to connect the sounds that make up the name of the picture.

th | ch

Mentally count the words

Count and write how many different words there are in the sentence.

1. "My mother is very beautiful".
   1   2   3 4   5

   [5] – words

2. The dog had the ball.

   [ ] – words

3. The wind blew off the girl's hat.

   [ ] – words

4. What kind of cake did we bake?

   [ ] – words

5. What is your brother's name?

   [ ] – words

6. I thought I saw a horse but it was a donkey.

   [ ] – words

7. My brother and my sister are studying in college.

   [ ] – words

8. We will go to school by bus.

   [ ] – words

9. He is under the chair.

   [ ] – words

10. The pigeon is on the big tree.

   [ ] – words

65

Mentally count the words

Count and write how many different words there are in the sentence.

1. I see the bus. $\boxed{4}$ – words

2. I put all my books in my bag. $\boxed{}$ – words

3. I am going home after the party. $\boxed{}$ – words

4. I think you are a good girl. $\boxed{}$ – words

5. What is your name? $\boxed{}$ – words

6. . I am going on a long walk with my sister. $\boxed{}$ – words

7. Please, let her play with your toys. $\boxed{}$ – words

8. This blanket is soft and warm. $\boxed{}$ – words

9. I will blow the candle out. $\boxed{}$ – words

10. When are you going home? $\boxed{}$ – words

66

Mentally count the words

Make and write a sentence according to the number of given words.

4 words → <u>Jack</u> <u>is</u> <u>very</u> <u>happy.</u>
          1 2 3   4

8 words →

6 words →

4 words →

7 words →

9 words →

5 words →

7 words →

Mentally count the words

Connect the sentence to the correct number of words.

1. I have a blue bag.

2. I am happy.

3. Turn off the TV before bed.

4. She is my friend.

5. My parents help me in every work.

6. We bought the new car with our credit card.

7. Don't run on the road it's too dangerous.

8. I can do different dance steps with this shiny red ribbon.

9. My father leaves the house and goes to work at his office.

10. I looked in the mirror and saw the skin on my forehead.

9 words

6 words

4 words

8 words

10 words

5 words

11 words

3 words

12 words

7 words

68

Omit a word **in a sentence**

What would remain if we removed the 3rd word from the sentence?

1. My uncle <u>was</u> in the club last week.

   My uncle in club last week.

2. It was very cold last night.

3. The old lady is not feeling well today.

4. I saw an airplane in the sky.

5. My mother brought me an apple and ice-cream.

6. An ant was drowning in the pond.

7. Herry will not graduate this year.

69

Omit a word in a sentence

What would remain if we removed the 3rd word from the sentence?

1. This movie is very funny.

   _____

2. Take your muddy shoes off.

   _____

3. The dog is running away!

   _____

4. Move this blue chair closer to the table.

   _____

5. We are going out to a dinner party.

   _____

6. This teddy bear is so cute.

   _____

7. My friend likes to read books.

Omit a word **in a sentence**

What would remain if we removed the 3rd word from the sentence?

1. My sock has a hole in it.

   _____

2. My sister and I are going to the movies.

   _____

3. I was born in October.

   _____

4. I love winter because of the snow.

   _____

5. Kelly used blueberry jam in her sandwich.

   _____

6. There was a huge crowd at the show.

   _____

7. Polly plays with her younger brother.

   _____

71

Omit a word in a sentence

What would remain if we removed the 3rd word from the sentence?

1. Please wait awhile.

   _____

2. They started working right away.

   _____

3. He spent money on his new bike.

   _____

4. Butter is made from milk.

   _____

5. The hare raced against the tortoise.

   _____

6. The dog wears a leash and a collar.

   _____

7. I like my cupcake with icing on top.

   _____

72

Substitute a word in a sentence

What would remain if we substituted the 3rd word of the sentence for the word "fat"?

1. The girls play football in the school play ground.

   The girls fat football in the school play ground.
   _____

2. Jack bought a new car.

   _____

3. The bell rang on time.

   _____

4. I like to eat pizza.

   _____

5. Look at my new computer.

   _____

6. The rhino has a sharp horn.

   _____

Substitute a word in a sentence

What would remain if we substituted the 3rd word of the sentence for the word "pin"?

1. We go to school on the school bus.

   _____

2. What color is that dress?

   _____

3. Green is my favorite color.

   _____

4. The tree in my yard has oranges.

   _____

5. I read a story book in my bed.

   _____

6. I want to eat some candies now.

   _____

Substitute a word in a sentence

What would remain if we substituted the 3rd word of the sentence for the word "fun"?

1. The mother's name is Kelly James.

    _____

2. Miles is going to the zoo.

    _____

3. The duck is yellow.

    _____

4. Can I feed your cat?

    _____

5. Can you see the gloves?

    _____

6. I can see a coconut tree on the beach.

    _____

75

Substitute a word in a sentence

What would remain if we substituted the 3rd word of the sentence for the word "pet"?

1. I am not sure about this question.

   _____

2. We have searched everywhere.

   _____

3. He was with his family and friends.

   _____

4. Did you see the monkey on the tree?

   _____

5. She waved at her brothers.

   _____

6. How do you do?

   _____

Separate written phrases **into words**

Read and separate the words in the sentences with lines.

1. ThesearethereasonswhyIdomywork.

   These/are/the/reasons/why/I/do/my/work.

2. WhatIwantforChristmas.

3. Theflowerswereformybestfriend.

4. Shewasfightingwithherfriend.

5. Pleasepackyourschoolbagproperly.

6. Thefloorinthehouseisveryclean.

77

Separate written phrases into words

Read and separate the words in the sentences with lines.

1. Ourscienceteacherismakingaverydifficulttest.

_____

2. Myyoungerbrotherisstartingschooltoday.

_____

3. Mile'swifeisgoingtoapartytodayinhernewcar.

_____

4. Wemadechocolatecakewithmybrothertoday.

_____

5. Ialwaysgotoworkbybus.

_____

6. Aplaneisflyingoverthecity.

_____

Separate written phrases into words

Read and separate the words in the sentences with lines.

1. Marywenttoschool.

_____

2. Thenapkinisplacedbesidethespoon.

_____

3. WearetravelingtoWashingtontomorrow.

_____

4. Ifeelsolonelywithoutyou.

_____

5. There'sabird'snestoutsidemyhouse.

_____

6. NobodycametothepartyexceptforPollyandMark.

_____

Separate written phrases into words

Read and separate the words in this sentence with lines.

1. ShecanspeakperfectSpanish.

_____

2. Heaskedmetohelphissister.

_____

3. Shetoldhimtowaitoutsideforonehour.

_____

4. Keepthistoyourself.

_____

5. Youarereallyagooddancer.

_____

6. Ilikeyourcompanyverymuch.

_____

80

Write a sentence with binomials

Write sentences with the given binomials.

1. give-take

   Every relationship requires lots of give and take.
   _____

2. time-again

   _____

3. alive-well

   _____

4. up-down

   _____

5. there-then

   _____

6. divide-rule

   _____

81

Write a sentence with **binomials**

Write sentences with the given binomials.

1. hustle-bustle

2. on-off

3. more-less

4. part-parcel

5. peace-quiet

6. sick-tired

82

Write a sentence with binomials

Write sentences with the given binomials.

1. safe-sound

_____

2. flying-night

_____

3. by-large

_____

4. bits-pieces

_____

5. home-dry

_____

6. wet-dry

_____

83

Write a sentence with **binomials**

Write sentences with the given binomials.

1. wine-dine

_____

2. home-hosed

_____

3. more-more

_____

4. husband-wife

_____

5. in-out

_____

6. rich-poor

_____

84

Spelling exercise for words

Understand the sound of the graphemes, then the name of the letters and circle it.

R	i	?	e	———————————	j	or	(d)

H	o	?	e	———————————	p	or	q
B	?	l	l	———————————	a	or	o
G	l	a	?	———————————	b	or	d
K	i	?	e	———————————	l	or	t
B	a	?	y	———————————	d	or	b
Y	e	a	?	———————————	r	or	s
S	h	o	?	———————————	q	or	p
G	l	a	?	———————————	b	or	d

85

Spelling exercise for words

Understand the sound of the graphemes and then fill in the blanks.

l o w	squ _ re	l _ fe
ska _ e	bl _ w	enj _ y
g _ ant	grad _	tin _
perf _ ct	ali _ e	dra _
won _ er	_ very	f _ mily
a _ so	b _ nd	ligh _
b _ ing	pe _ ce	s _ ecial
_ ast	_ dea	g _ ound
mo _ ey	seco _ d	agai _
s _ op	loo _	_ oot

86

Spelling exercise for words

Write the words two times.

west ✔ _____ west _____ | _____ west _____

chair ◯ _____ | _____

bath ◯ _____ | _____

parents ◯ _____ | _____

table ◯ _____ | _____

room ◯ _____ | _____

angle ◯ _____ | _____

ticket ◯ _____ | _____

jacket ◯ _____ | _____

shirt ◯ _____ | _____

87

Spelling exercise for words

Write the correct word.

laram _alarm_

ookb _____

hsfi _____

atrwe _____

tje _____

ttbole _____

igtf _____

nisal _____

ihckc _____

lidch _____

laram _____

hta _____

hleaw _____

odynke _____

88

Activities with rhymes

Circle the words in each row that have the same rhyming sound.

cook	(book)	moon	case	well
flute	feet	dress	cute	best
fun	red	hut	cake	bun
row	toe	bow	tea	ball
hen	fan	kite	pen	wet
wish	dish	wise	nice	three
wing	ten	ring	stick	bag
tub	fight	sky	rub	pie

89

Substitution of syllables

Replace the 2nd syllable of the word with 'th'.

terrible	elephant
_____	_____
fingers	president
_____	_____
freedom	butterfly
_____	_____
reading	football
_____	_____
playground	popcorn
_____	_____

9

Activities with rhymes

Draw a line to match the same rhyming sound.

fall	rat
cat	cook
pine	car
book	train
hand	pad
star	tall
rain	band
mad	fine

90

Activities with rhymes

Fill in the blanks with the correct rhyming words.

sat ➡	_____mat_____	, _____hat_____	, _____bat_____
fin ➡	_____	, _____	, _____
well ➡	_____	, _____	, _____
job ➡	_____	, _____	, _____
light ➡	_____	, _____	, _____
good ➡	_____	, _____	, _____
bake ➡	_____	, _____	, _____
class ➡	_____	, _____	, _____
air ➡	_____	, _____	, _____
slow ➡	_____	, _____	, _____
cot ➡	_____	, _____	, _____
ship ➡	_____	, _____	, _____

91

Activities with rhymes

Match the same rhyming words.

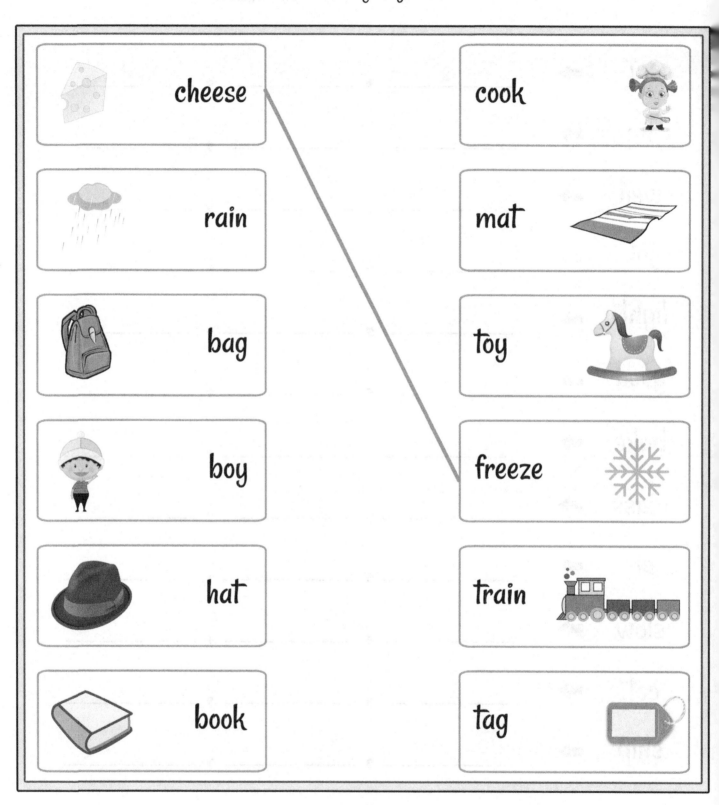

cheese

rain

bag

boy

hat

book

cook

mat

toy

freeze

train

tag

92

Phonological Awareness

Scrabble spelling: Build and write your words in the given boxes.

A	B	C	D	E	F	G	H	I	J	K	L	M	N
O	P	Q	R	S	T	U	V	W	X	Y	Z		

words	points
1.	
2.	
3.	
4.	
5.	
6.	
7.	
8.	
9.	
10.	

93

Phonological Awareness

Make different words from the given set of letters and write them in the boxes.

L	H	T	E	A	N	E	P

1. ANT ✔
2.
3.
4.
5.
6.
7.
8.
9.
10.

94

Phonological Awareness

Word search.

APPLE	PIG	PUMPKIN	SEAL	AIRPLANE
LAMP	CUPCAKE	SCHOOL	CLOCK	BIRD

A	P	P	L	E	X	Z	E	R	T
I	I	I	L	O	P	Q	W	A	D
R	G	F	B	N	C	L	O	C	K
P	U	I	S	E	A	L	A	H	M
L	R	F	V	B	N	M	J	U	D
A	T	S	C	H	O	O	L	D	K
N	A	Z	X	V	B	K	A	F	C
E	R	N	L	Q	E	X	M	B	U
D	G	B	I	R	D	Y	P	F	P
Y	C	X	D	E	H	K	Q	A	C
N	M	F	D	U	T	M	G	B	A
P	U	M	P	K	I	N	U	B	K
N	H	J	Y	K	L	E	D	F	E

95

Phonological Awareness

Say aloud the name of the given pictures and write the beginning sound you hear.

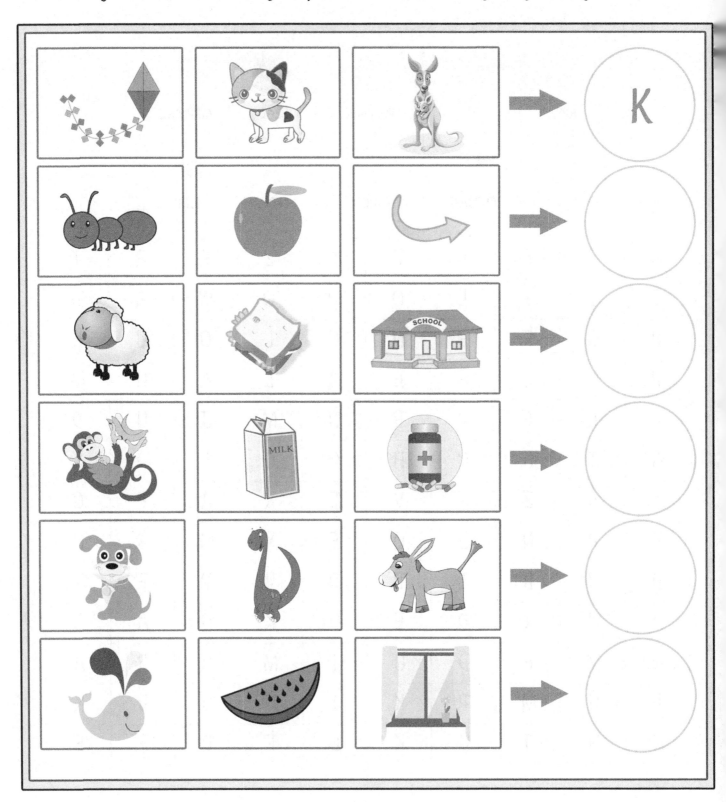

Visual discrimination of graphemes

Color the boxes with the correct letters.

Color the boxes with the letter – b

b	d	d	b	b	d

Color the boxes with the letter – d

d	d	b	d	b	d

Color the boxes with the letter – b

b	b	d	d	b	b

Color the boxes with the letter – d

b	b	d	d	b	d

Visual discrimination of graphemes

Match the patterns.

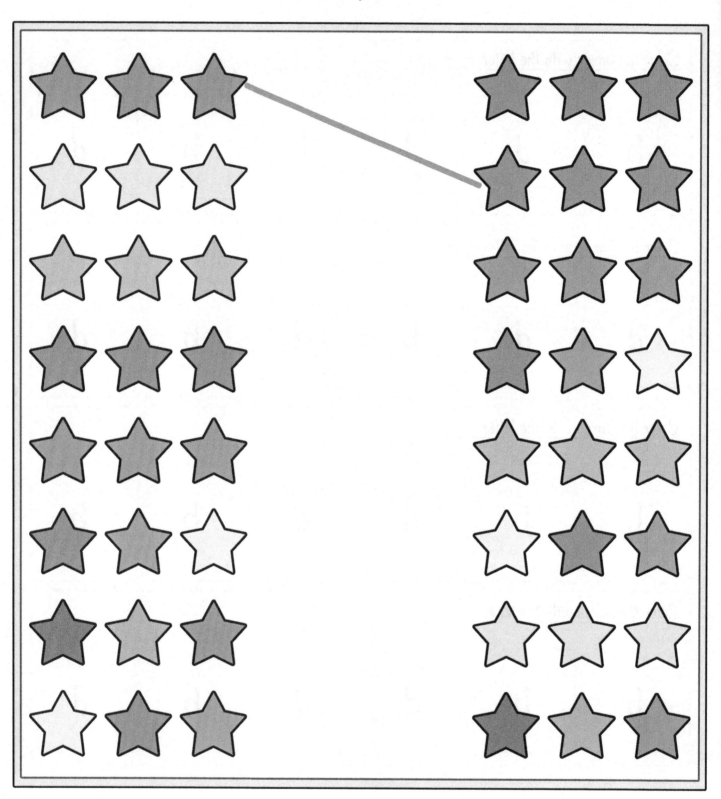

Visual discrimination of graphemes

Match the identical pictures

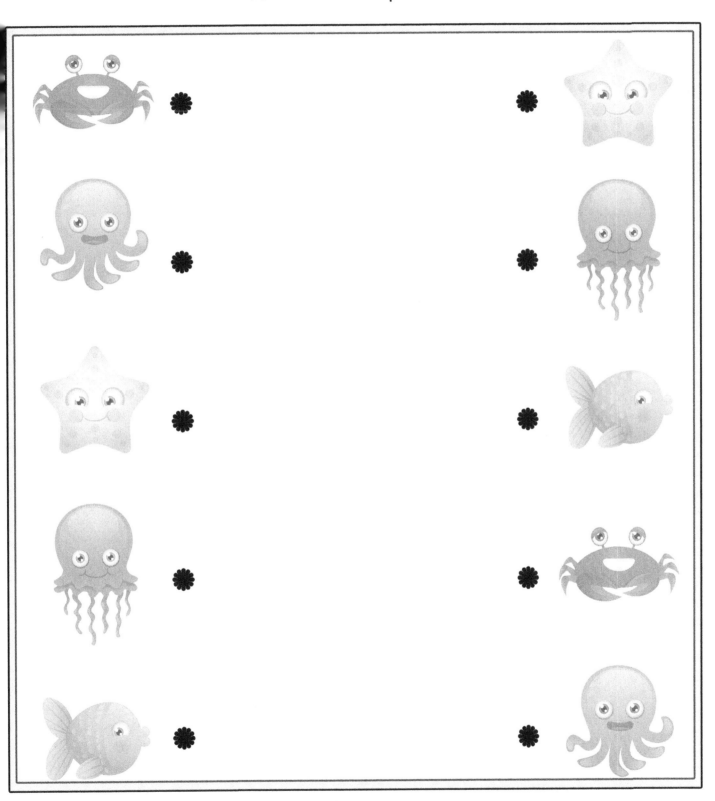

Visual discrimination of graphemes

Find the odd one out.

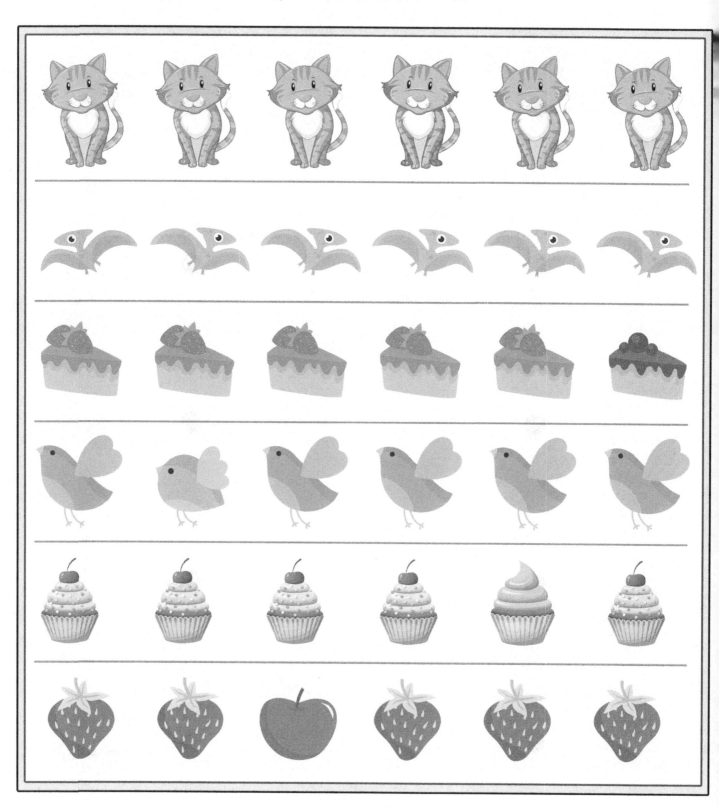

100

Find other Brainchild Books on Amazon

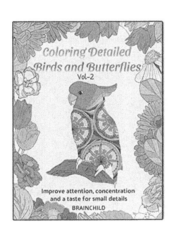

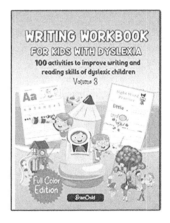

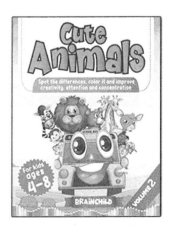

Made in United States
North Haven, CT
26 October 2024

59442968R00063